Spanish Flamenco Dance Reference Guide

2nd Edition

by

Alicia Morena - di Palma

Spanish

Flamenco

Dance Reference Guide

2nd Edition

Alicia Morena - di Palma

SPANISH FLAMENCO DANCE REFERENCE GUIDE, 2ND EDITION

The photo credits section for this book is on page 76 and is considered an extension of the copyright page.

Morena - di Palma, Alicia
Spanish Flamenco Dance Reference Guide, 2nd Edition/ Alicia Morena - di Palma.

Library of Congress Cataloging-in-Publication Data

Printed in the United States of America
1st Edition   1999
2nd Edition   2002

10 9 8 7 6 5 4 3

Publisher's note. Neither the movements of this dance program nor any dance or exercise program should be followed without first consulting a health care professional. If you have any special conditions requiring attention, you should consult your health care professional regularly regarding possible modification of the program contained in this book.

Additional copies of this book maybe obtained through the distributor:

Wood Designs, Inc.
PO Box 1790
New Waverly, TX 77358-1790
1-877-612-8306
http://FlamencoGuide.com

Or you can contact the author at Author@FlamencoGuide.com

To Roberto Andrés, Rosa Durán and El Sevillano

I remember the tingling high after those intense lessons at Estudio Calderón on Calle Atocha in Madrid.

Afterwards, I went with my teacher Rosa Durán, and guitarist Roberto Andrés and his mentor El Sevillano, to a nearby *flamenco bar*. Here we drank café *solo* from tiny cups and laughed and shared the affection of this discipleship.

I dedicate my book to Roberto, Rosa, and El Sevillano with appreciation for their gifts which keep giving and receiving.

Table of Contents

Illustrations

IN MEMORIAM: ROSA DURÁN (1925-2000)

To Rosa,
who still sees and hears the authentic flamenco, I owe you everything that has made me a much better creative person and dancer. You inspired me, especially in times of silent communications across the pond. How joyous were the human sharings of your "vamos al campo," our outings with flamenco families in Roberto's Citroën, the silly skits over cafecitos in a roadside café, and spontaneous floral exchanges at Estudio Calderón - my tulipanes for you, and your violets for me
Adios, Preciosa!

She was the very *"figura"* I wanted to study with after reading Quintana and Floyd's *Qué Gitano!* in the San Francisco State University library. Roberto was being transferred to UNIVAC Spain to work on Iberia Airline's materials system and we were going home to the muse. From those years of study and friendship with Rosa, *El Sevillano*, and the *flamenco* artists of their milieu, I learned that *flamenco's* survival is really tested away from the source, and that source is always carried within you. *Flamenco* becomes the metaphor of survival with love, an attitude, a technique, a dance of courage and catharsis for wherever one is in time and space: *"aquí estoy yo!"*

Los Tarantos had been playing at *Teatro Reina Victoria* in Madrid soon after our arrival and it featured Rosa Durán. From textbook to Madrid reality and with our jet lag subsiding, we took in the Sunday matinee, comparing the dance attributes of our favorite Amaya and Durán before the curtain. They were already considered *"figuras"* or legends in their time, one the "queen of the Gypsies," the other "empress of the *jondo* lineage." Rosa, part *paya* and non-*paya* (*gitana*), floated across the stage in a sharp, footwork dialog with Périco el del Lunar, and told the Gypsy Romeo and Juliet drama with her face, voice, and entire *flamenco* dance body. Her eyes focused and her head followed every move of her body with restraint, undulation, and sensual elegance. Her line pulsated with power. Like Amaya, she could bridge feminine and masculine energy with mystery in her personification of the dance: the sensational *Zapateado* of El Estampío presented in the *bata de cola*, and *peteneras* arms and feet rhythmically portraying the legend of Paterna, without superstition, and with a new esthetic value.

I luckily found Rosa's telephone number and she granted me an interview at Estudio Calderón. It was destiny meeting her in that space, like a gossamer skrim between us that opened up to the light and our faces. She walked around me in silence after my brief, excited introduction, then stopped in front of me and looked well into my face. Suddenly she smiled a smile of enormous delight. Her face took me back to my childhood, to blended oriental and occidental aspects and something compelling of India, long ago.

If I wanted to study her Gypsy *siguiriyas* I was to wear a *bata de cola*[1] and learn to use the most tiny *castanets* called *palillos*[2]. These I did not have and she offered to loan me both until I could get my own, to which she added *"es mas profundo como asi."* She turned to Maestro José at the desk, reserved studio space and announced, holding my chin: *"mire la cara bonita y la cara de Rosita y gitanilla."*

There were over two years of intense discipleship, and she said to me in class once that of the many applicants, I was her only chosen student outside of Iberia and her last, like the passage of *jondo* dancing from Spain. The daughter of Isabelita de Jerez and the niece of El Marruro, a famous Gypsy singer of *siguiriyas* and *tientos*, Rosa had been given the torch by her teachers at an early age, Angel Pericet in Madrid and El Estampío of Jerez. She danced in street fairs, for Gypsy rituals, and during the big fiestas featured by aristocracy. Rosa Durán toured in Europe and England, was soloist for Fernán Casares' famed <u>Zambra</u> in Madrid, and was the featured artist in the Pavilion of Spain at the New York World's Fair in 1965. She is the recipient of national awards from the United States, France and Italy, and was awarded the *Premio Nacional de España de Baile* in 1962.

After touring, marriage, the death of her singer husband, and raising a daughter, whom she coached and choreographed for, she took on solo engagements when not ill from liver damage owing to the deprivation of the war years (1936-1938), taught selected classes at dance studios, and kept the company of an aging duchess, having become a personal *flamenco* dancer and teacher to the House of Alba for many years. Rosa purchased a *piso* (a flat) near the Plaza de Toros in Madrid by winning the national lottery one year. She lived on the top floor with her memorable artifacts, her daughter Cristina studying foreign languages, and an African grey parrot who could mimic the words and tones of the *flamenco cantes* Rosa played daily and repeated *"cariño mio"* incessantly. This *piso* was the scene of talk and *tapas* over the trumpets and roar of the Plaza de Toros below.

Rosa seldom talked about the *flamenco* art, keeping away from its gossip, and was more concerned about the life of the artist – the challenges, the struggles, the survival with style (that ¡Aire!). She trusted only movement, and each expressive move or *paso* she danced and taught had a life of its own, and often dancer and dance became one. She stressed often that in the communication between guitarist and dancer, the dancer becomes the "musician," and the guitarist, the "dancer."

I heard of Rosa's passing from a dance student who read about it in a Japanese journal. Five years before, a friend of mine in Spain visited her and the widow of El Sevillano living together outside of Madrid. The visit revealed a fine mind rather lost without that strong, deep, resonant voice, a body ailing, and intermittent *flamenco* memories. She had met them at the door, then disappeared, only to return fully made-up for the stage.

Rosa Durán knew about *jondo's* forgotten legacy in modern times, one that often leaves cultural inheritances behind. She belonged to another age of *flamenco* that drew its sustenance from *"el principio del gitano"*. Her telephone would ring off the hook after a revival of her works on Spanish National Television, and yet no one ever heard of Rosa Durán in the 1980's at a quaint restaurant in Chinchón, famous for Chinchón Dulce.

Rosa Durán's artistry was like no other in style, expression, use of compás, and the *jondo* line. *Flamenco* was her whole life in joy, sadness, and in between. It was her invocation and her benediction to her creator and for all those who were privileged to experience her creations.

---

[1] The Rosa Durán style of *bata de cola* and *corpiño* (a bodice with ¾ sleeves to the elbow like East Indian costuming) was sewn by Señora Costa of Madrid.
[2] Rosa sold me her first professional pair of *castanets* crafted for her by the renown guitar maker José Ramirez.

PREFACE

This syllabus is both a reference source and required reading for students enrolled in Alicia Morena's classes and workshops. This is not a detailed user manual and no videos or audio cassettes accompany the syllabus. The author believes that real-time modeling of the dance techniques, line, expression, choreography, costuming, and culture allows for effective interfaces, reflective learning, and constructive correction on the spot. The syllabus acts as a springboard for further research in the study and practice of Spanish *flamenco* dance.

This syllabus is available to students and teachers of other schools and styles of *flamenco* and all dance disciplines are invited to use it.

LA GUITARRA

Empieza el llanto
de la guitarra.
Se rompen las copas
de la madrugada.

FEDERICO GARCÍA LORCA

PONDER THIS

Many of us paint and dance and sign or play the guitar. Others of us restore cars, do needlepoint and cook wonderful dinners. And we use our imagination and creativity to do it— the same way artists do. But there are real differences in the creative work we do and the art produced by an artist. The important one lies in the intent of the process. A work of art has ambitious intentions. Artists aspire to create new forms, reveal emotional truth, explore the unexplored. They long to reach an audience at the deepest levels of meaning with their work.

IF IMAGINATION AND CREATIVITY ALONE MAKE ART, WE COULD ALL BE ARTISTS.

It takes an awesome imagination, a gifted talent, an original mind and consuming desire to overcome the seduction of technique, materials or craft—to make art. Some art is controversial. Some unfathomable. Much of it is beautiful and sensitive and makes us feel deeply. Few people like it all, nor should they. Art is too personal for that. But if what we make does not intend to be art, we can still share in the experience of imagining and creating with every artist. What a remarkable process creating is—giving back more, the more we risk.

THE NEW YORK FOUNDATION FOR THE ARTS

TIENTOS dancer on backyard stage

"In the dance, the spirit of the thing is inherited; what can be acquired is plasticity, geometry..."

Caballero Bonald

I.   INTRODUCTION

Historical Background

Spanish *flamenco* dancing has its roots in a multicultural origin: the Moorish presence on the Iberian Peninsula; the Sephardic/Ladino influences in Córdoba; the arrival of gypsy tribes in the middle of the 15th Century; the new ideas brought back to Spain from voyages of discovery and conquest; the popular domestic dancing of the 17th Century grafted on to courtly dances through professional studies (Andalucian with Greco-Roman and French); and the appearance from 1850 onward of a song, music, and dance form known as *flamenco.*

It is a relatively recent and eclectic form, combining the elements of Andalucian folkdance, song, and music with its oldest source - the liturgical and esoteric jondo dancing. The *flamenco* dancing that started in smoke-filled *cafés*, *cantantes*, taverns, and *bodegas* has found modern venues in theaters and concert halls, museums, outdoor festivals, hotels, restaurants, and bars (*tablao*). It had its fondest cultural supporters in García-Lorca and Manuel de Falla, in the artists of France and Russia, and on the college and university campuses in the USA during the 30's, 40's and 50's. Today, *flamenco* "fusion" spices modern musical and dance idioms, and has a global following led by the Japanese.

Overview of Dance Material

The student dancer will be introduced to a variety of Spanish dances that include the *jota* dances of Aragon and Valencia, dances from the Spanish classical school, and the *flamenco* of Andalucia in Southern Spain. He or she will become aware of the characteristics of each dance, the historical and cultural origins, and differences between intimate performances of the dances, and stage and commercial dancing *(ambiente)*. The emphasis will be on basic rhythms called *compás*, centering, balance, line, feet positions and footwork, arm and hand work, and dancing with the control and expression of the face, head, neck, shoulders, torso, and hips. Female students are required to wear full, long skirts, long-sleeved leotards, tights, and leg warmers for extra knee protection and warmth. Male students should wear a comfortable top with long sleeves and loose trousers. Traditional *flamenco* shoes or dance boots should be worn for proper footwear support. A large dance shawl *(mantón de Manila),* a fan *(abanico),* and castanets *(castañuelas or palillos)* are implements necessary for learning certain dances. (See also, Appendix.)

Characteristics of *Flamenco*

Flamenco comes from the Arabic *felah mengu* meaning a Moor, peasant, or soldier-in-flight. The essence of this multicultural dance form is as follows:

- A function of the individual or solo dancer.

- Introverted movements with reduced dance area, and a focal point not at the audience, but from the place where the dancer stands inclined toward the earth.

- An abstract dance, in which the dancer interprets the music and leads the guitarist, with liberty of expression and a capacity for improvisation.

- A mood of ecstasy, rapture, or a trance of concentrated power and intensity, manifested in both postured and highly energized action.

- An obedience to the structured count pattern of the *compás,* in a repetition balanced by cycles of tension and release.

- An understanding of *flamenco* choreography as the inherited patterns of a particular dance culture; a lineage passed from teacher-to-student, family-to-family, instilling a tradition.

References

Caballero, Bonald, J. M. *Andalusian Dances.* Taylor & Francis, 1959.
    ISBN: 0800223969.
Claramunt, A. P. *El Arte del Baile Flamenco.* Ediciones Poligrafa, 1977.
    ISBN: 8434302438.
de la Peñia, T. M. *Teoria y Practica del Baile Flamenco*. Noguer, Madrid, 1969.

II.   ANDALUCIAN DANCES: JONDO AND FLAMENCO

Alegrías

Alegrías, meaning happiness, merriment, or gaiety, is a dance of the *jondo*Lineage. This popular dance originating in Cádiz, encourages the artistic expression of the dancer in a 12-beat count that is identical to the s*oleares*. However, the *alegrías* is faster, accentuating the musical structure of the bright major chords rather than the melancholy minor chords. Some researchers cite that the *alegrías* was influenced by the *jotas aragonesas. Romeras, mirabrás,* and *caracoles* are related dances differing in the accented rhythm, atmosphere, and characteristic expression. The *alegrías* is technically difficult to perform and is best expressed in the choreographies of El Estampío, Rosa Durán, and Vicente Escudero.

Bulerías

The birthplace of the *bulerías* is probably Jerez de la Frontera and its name comes from the verb *burlar* meaning to "jest". It shares the same 12-count *compás* of the *alegrías* and *soleá*, but its syncopation, tempo, and underlying counter-time suggest a lighter, friendly teasing, building to a manic burst of rhythm. There is much verbal and musical support from the *cuadro*, a semicircle of dancers, guitarists, and singers. It is a dance in which one is encouraged to outdo the other or one's self, relax with the beat, and show off. The *bulerías* has a complex rhythmic structure and lends itself nicely to improvisation. The lyrics for the song can be humorous, cute, proud, sentimental, and sometimes ironically sad.

Farruca

Farruca, meaning brave and courageous, is a popular *flamenco* dance traditionally performed by men. The woman's expression of it was made famous by Carmen Amaya. The author adapted her choreography from Teresita Osta, who was taught her *farruca* by El Chino, Carmen Amaya's father. A typical *farruca* costume is the *traje corto* with pants or a skirt as shown in the adjacent picture. The dance's origin is probably Asturian or Galician as the song, rarely sung, indicates. The Andalucian Gypsies converted the folk song into a *flamenco* dance befitting their taste and temperament. The *farruca* has been influenced by the *tangos* of Cádiz, shares the same *compás* of 4s, and is sometimes described as a stylization of a bullfighter's attitudes. The dance has a static, grave, cadenced quality and is tinged with sadness. As the *farruca* moves to its *tanguillo* ending, the song or *cante* tells about lost love perpetuated in nature. The song translates as follows:

A maiden in Galicia

Bitterly she cried
For her beloved had died
The one who played the bagpipes for her.
Oh high the lemon
Low, the olive.
High grows the lemon
Lemon tree of my life and love.

Tango Gitano

The cultural origins of the *tango* are uncertain and varied: Argentinean; the names of Latin musical instruments; the songs of Northern Spain and Africa. The Spanish gypsy developed *tango* singing, which is considered one of the oldest and basic *cantes* or songs. They express a manic or lighter side of life, as well as a brooding or serious sense of it. The *tango* dance interprets both moods with restraint and a driving straight forward rhythm of evenly accented 4s. *Tango* dancing is well-marked and carries the ancient cultural sentiments of the Hindu Bayadere in its sensuous and ritual movements.

Guajiras and Colombianas

Guajiras refers to a peasant, a native of Guantanamo, a lady or gentleman, and is also a popular Cuban song. In the 16th century, the Spanish *conquistadores* brought this tropical melody back to the ports of Andalucia where the song was adapted to *flamenco* music for the guitar in 6/8 and 3/4 time. This *flamenco* piece is known as *ida y vuelta* or round trip. In the Mayan language of the Yucatan Indians, *guajira* means lady and *guajiro* means gentleman.

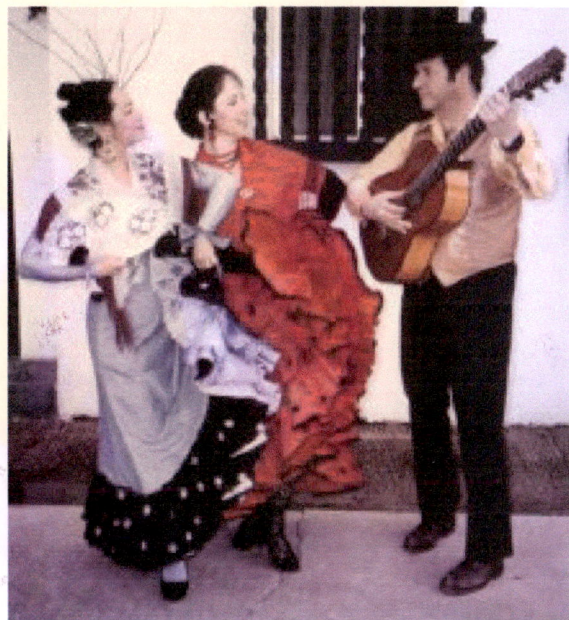

These words were also used by the Indians of Colombia and Venezuela, whose language is related to the Araucan Indians. Usually, the songs deal with Cuba and Cubans, the Spanish, Indians and Mulattos. The words are sometimes racy or poetical, about fatalistic love, or fate and fortune. The *guajiras* is an elegant dance form suggesting the sweetness of tropical fruit, and the sultry, sensuous qualities of a Havana night. The characteristic of the dance is the walk (*paseo)*, accented by *pellizcos*, literally "a pinch of salt that flavors the dancing" with movements of the hips, neck, head, face, and shoulders. The dance is performed with and without *castanets*, and this choreographic version includes the *colombianas*, danced with a fan. (Carmen Amaya sang and danced a *colombianas*, a *flamenco* dedication to Colombia and the *cumbias*, on her American tours, accompanied by Sabicas on the guitar.)

Jota Aragonesa

The *jota aragonesa* folk dance is from the province of Aragon in Northern Spain. There are also *jotas* of the Basque provinces and of Valencia. It is a dance performed by couples, in groups, or solo, with singers and musicians. The *jota* is characteristically very graceful, exuberant, and athletic. The song or *canción* in the *jota aragonesa* is expressed by waltz-like steps throughout the dance. *Castanets*, finger-snapping, and tambourines are used to keep the rhythm   (1,2,3/4,5,6   or 1 and a 2 and 3). The *zapatillas* or slipper dance shoes are trimmed in black for a *jota* from Aragon, and those of Navarra would have a red trim.

Peteneras

The music of the *peteneras* echoes medieval Spain and the song and dance is about the girl from Paterna de la Ribera, *Cádiz,* or the Jewess from the Judería in Córdoba. *Peteneras* songs are dissimilar from the other *cantes flamencos,* and the distinct lyrics *(letras)* have been passed from generation to generation within certain groups. In the Aramean idiom (Jesus Christ's native tongue), *Pathe Erneer* is a singing introduction to prayer, or primitive singing. Popular in the 17th and 18th centuries, the *petenera* is still performed with some reserve, as it is considered rather superstitious; the legend has it that the singer who created this song met a tragic end.

Romance de Amor (Romance Anónimo)

Romance Anónimo is a classical guitar piece by an unknown composer. The dance has five movements in a pattern of AA, BB, and A, or five verses or *coplas* of the dance. An original choreography, it expresses the romantic spirit of the Spanish court and country life and integrates *flamenco* and classical stylizations, as well as, *Escuela Bolera, Verdial,* and *Zapatilla* techniques. This dance shows the use of the large Spanish fan *(pericóna)*, and moves in waltz time.

Sevillanas

Sevillanas is a popular dance typical of Sevilla and all of Andalucia in southern Spain. It is especially in vogue for Spanish people during the *Feria de Sevilla*. The dance was derived from the *Seguidillas Manchegas* of Castilla in central Spain. So infectious is the *sevillanas* rhythm, that at the drop of a Spanish *sombrero* it will be danced by couples of all ages dressed in colorful, traditional costumes. At the week long *Feria* in April, work is ignored and people dance the *sevillanas* around the clock. The *sevillanas* is very demanding when performed in the classical style. The measured detail of the choreography is best learned in dance academies. The *sevillanas* song *(cante)*, like the guitar accompaniment and *castanets*, is an important expressive ingredient to maintain the characteristic count *(compás)*. The exacting foot movements, graceful arm work, and tantalizing *castanets* should flow together in the *compás* of 1-2-3, 4-5-6.

TORRE del ORO
SEVILLANAS

2
Torre del Oro,
donde las sevillanas,
donde las sevillanas,
donde las sevillanas,
¡y olé!,
juegan al toro.

3
Tierra de luna,
donde las sevillanas,
donde las sevillanas,
donde las sevillanas,
¡y olé!,
tienen su cuna.

Siguiriyas

The word *siguiriya* (or *seguiriya*) is a composite of *sequir* and *siguiendo*, meaning to spring from, to accompany, to pursue a course of personal action, and to continue on one's way. *Siguiriyas* are the most profoundly emotional element of *flamenco* dancing, a complex form to express authentic feelings. The *siguiriya* acknowledges feelings of pent-up anger, persecution, betrayal, denied liberty and love, and tenderness toward a companion in misery. It mourns and releases the sentiment in an intensity of 12 characteristically marked beats (1´2´3´123´ 456´), driving away death which stalks life. Rosa Durán's dance focuses on the expressive face and hands moving in concentric circles like the opening and closing of the lotus flower. Dressed in black for absorbed emotion and red-orange reflecting an appetite for living, she becomes a moving tree with arms branching skyward and feet rooted in the earth. Her feet and small *castanets (palillos)*, that sound like tongue-clicking and finger-snapping, are the solemn rhythm keepers. The long dress train, called a *bata de cola*, sweeps away airy tears, cleaning up any vestige of self-pity. (See cover costume.)

Soleares or Soleá

The *soleares* or *soleá* evolved from the deep song *(Cante Jondo)* of the same name and is a relative of the *Polos* and *Cañas flamenco* dances. *Soleares* is a Gypsy mispronunciation of the word *soledad/soledades*, meaning solitude or loneliness. Alone, the dancer transforms the mood, moving from pensiveness to sprightliness. A strict *compás* of 12 counts is controlled by well-maintained countertime. The restraint and vehemence of movement and footwork unburden

the self caught-up-with-the-self, and a kind of psychic humor evolves within the dance. *Soleares* probably developed as a distinct dance from the gypsy quarter of Triana in the early 19th century. The dance form spread through Sevilla and Cádiz, with variations in style. La Macarrona (Juana Vargas), her predecessor, Josefa Vargas, and La Mejorana (Rosario Monje) were creators of the soleares in the female, *jondo*-Gypsy lineage.[1]

Tientos

The *tientos* are very similar to the slow gypsy t*angos* with an identical *compás*, structure and song verses often interchanged. The basic difference lies in the manner of musical accent; the guitar is accentuated on the first beat of the 4 count. *Tiento* beats are prolonged and shortened, giving the dance a perspective of remoteness and profundity. This is a feminine dance of Moorish origin with sensual arm work and appropriate, non-tedious footwork.

> *"Authentic Andalucian dancing keeps intact the oldest values of the primitive, eternal dance, the dance which is born and bursts forth a stormy need of the heart"*

José Caballero

---

[1] Dancers La Malena, La Macorrona, La Sordita, and Rosita Durán, and singers Manuel Torres and Antonio Chacón --all of the *"Raza cañi,"* shared the same birthplace; Jerez.

A Regal *Flamenco* Posture, *¡Aquí, Estoy Yo!* (Here I Am!)
(American Dancer and Choreographer, Agnes de Mille)

"Dancing is not just moving,
It is thinking."
Alexandra Danilova

III.   BASIC ELEMENTS OF SPANISH *FLAMENCO* MOVEMENTS

Essential Attitudes Reflected in the Dance Movements

Just as feet have a determined function in *flamenco* as rhythm keepers and are placed artistically in *jondo* dancing, the movements of the head, torso, and arms are used to convey inner expression. These sentiments or attitudes reside in the movements of the body and can be described as:

- A sensual quality, as in primitive and oriental dance, an expression of vitality; also closed movements, concentricity, and an attitude of restraint.

- An emotional attitude that tests the sensibility of the artist to carry the intent (solitude, romantic pursuit, loss, personal catharsis, happiness, clowning, teasing, etc.) uninterrupted through the dance. The body expresses these sensations through movements of the head, intense expressions of the face, held poses, foreshortened furious movements, static poses of strength, smooth undulations, delicate movements of the arms, and tasteful flirtations of the shoulders.

- A profundity or mystery, perceived as a special type of movement – pervasive, inimitable, and ethereal.

1.   Warm-ups

These exercises help to develop isolated muscle groups, extensions, and endurance. A properly warmed up body helps to reduce undue straining and accidents. Start with deep breathing and meditation techniques, and work slowly, to maintain your breathing evenly in and out.

> ### Lao-Tzu
>
> Some say that my teaching is nonsense.
> Others call it lofty but impractical.
> But to those who have looked inside themselves,
> This nonsense makes perfect sense.
> And to those who put it into practice,
> This loftiness has roots that go deep.
>
> I have just three things to teach:
> Simplicity, patience, compassion.
> These three are your greatest treasures.
> Simple in actions and in thoughts,
> You return to the source of being.
> Patient with both friends and enemies,
> You accord with the way things are.
> Compassionate toward yourself,
> You reconcile all beings in the world.

Young *Sevillana's* Stretch

a.   Neck

Circular Rolls: Roll neck slowly to the left and right, front and back, changing direction. (Note that cracking sounds relate to tight, tense muscles. Do not attempt this if you have had a neck injury, swelling, severe headache, or fever.)

Neck stretch: Using both hands, one on the head, and one on the shoulder, press your head down gently and forward, with eyes upward, toward the left shoulder. Repeat for the right side. This is helpful for regaining curvature in the neck.

b.   Neck, Abdomen and Lower Back (mime exercise for flexibility of the neck and torso)

Starting with the head and neck, roll forward. Using the eyes to mark space, move downward, vertebra by vertebra toward the floor, tucking in the abdomen and tucking buttocks. Return upward in like manner. Then move the head backward, gradually arching back, arms loosely hung, and left foot extended front. Return to upright position slowly; repeat on right side.

c.   Sides and Flank

Side stretches: Stretch to the left side, with the right arm curved at ear level, reaching to the opposite side, then returning to the waist, right side. Maintain left hand at waist, feet spaced evenly apart, and expend energy through fingertips of hands. Repeat on right side.

d.   Shoulders and Arms

Shoulder - arm rotation: Hold right shoulder with left hand (maintain level of right shoulder) while rotating the right arm from its socket, first inward, then outward. Repeat on left side.

Chest-back, arms swing: Swing arms out to front of chest and then to the back, then clasp shoulders, slightly rocking left to right. Clasp palms to the lower back at the base of the spine pulling shoulders gently down to the left and to the right. Bring clasped arms and hands up from back and above head while bending head to touch the left knee. Release hands and arms and gently drop neck and head down toward floor; relax and hang there like a limp ragdoll. Finally, grasp the ankles with both hands, carefully bending the head toward the feet. Come up slowly to the upright position, moving both arms out in curved formation. Simultaneously step to the left and bring left arm down to left side slowly; repeat on the right side to finish exercise (head and eyes follow movements). Repeat entire exercise on the right side.

Jazz arm-rolls: With the head and eyes focused on the right arm elongated and stretched to the fingertips, roll arm forward and backward/forward and forward/backward and backward. Repeat on the left side by changing feet orientation; left foot pointed out in the starting direction. Repeat with both arms outstretched, using varying combinations of the roll; head and eyes focused forward.

Hindu arm extensions: Pose both hands with thumb and pointer finger in closed circle. Extend both arms with finished hand pose, horizontally right and left. Pull in the right extended arm; palm upward, straightened elbow, with hand still posed. The left arm is stationary with hand posed three fingers upward, circled thumb and forefinger. Right foot is posed with toes upward, on heel, and the left leg in slight *plié*. Head and eyes focus on the extensions of the pulled-in arms. Repeat on left side.

e.   Hands, Wrists and Fingers

Rotation: Rotate wrists in circles, inside and outside, fisted and open hand and finger formation. Do the same with each of the ten fingers. Maintain feet in the Spanish/*flamenco* 3rd position and extended arms and hands at same level, rotating them together from front to back, without straining. Complete movement by clasping the hands together in back and pulling them downward gently from the shoulders. Alter the wrist rotations and arm movements using thumbs of the hands up and down (this helps to toughen and lengthen the underside arm muscles).

2.   Basic Spanish/*Flamenco* Dance Positions

a. (1st Position) Preparation: Heels of feet together. Drawing energy from the earth beneath, maintain first position with arms at waist level, at front, with hands relaxed, fingers slightly parted, opposing.

b. (2nd Position) Step out to the right from the first position moving with your eyes in that direction, head and feet together. Both arms are extended out as a large half circle with elbows held. The feet are evenly apart in open second position, and the line of the body is fully centered.

c. (3rd Position) Place right foot to the right, "side–front," leaving the second position. Side–front means orienting the body to the front, but arm/leg/foot is angled slightly off to the left. Right arm is aligned with the right foot at chest level and the left arm is above the head, with elbow slightly back of the ear (ear level).

d. (4th Position) Move left foot over right foot and balance on the ball of the foot *(punta)*. Right arm moves up center to join left arm, in the air, above the head.

e. (5th Position) Make a half-turn *(media vuelta)* going right, returning to the starting position facing forward. Both arms move on the outside down to waist level and are crossed, as the eyes spot to execute the half turn.

f. (6th Position) Bien Planta. Put the right foot forward in *punta pie*. When the back (left) foot has executed a sound with the flat of the foot (*planta*), the arms and hands are released back into a third position placement.

Repeat a, b, c, d, e, f, going left (L).

3.   Footwork Table

The *flamenco* "foot" consists of the heel of the foot *(tacón)*; toe and ball of the foot *(punta)*; and the flat of the foot *(planta)*. Please read the one-word instruction from left to right for each lettered line in the following table:

FOOTWORK SEQUENCE	LEFT FOOT	RIGHT FOOT
A	FLAT	FLAT FLAT
B	FLAT	
A	FLAT	FLAT FLAT
B	FLAT FLAT	FLAT FLAT
C	FLAT	
A	FLAT FLAT	FLAT FLAT
A	TOE HEEL	FLAT FLAT
B	FLAT	

FOOTWORK SEQUENCE	LEFT FOOT	RIGHT FOOT
A	AND TOE	FLAT
B	FLAT	FLAT
C	FLAT	
A	FLAT	SCUFF (with full foot, a drag)
B	HEEL	FLAT
A	FLAT	SCUFF
B	HEEL	FLAT
C	SCUFF	HEEL
D	FLAT	SCUFF
E	HEEL	FLAT
A	HEEL	HEEL
B	HEEL	HEEL
A	SCUFF	SCUFF
B	HEEL	HEEL
A	HEEL	TOE HEEL
B	HEEL	FLAT

4. *El Juego* (Warm-up Set)

Positioning of feet: Place left foot down *(planta)* and follow with right ball of foot *(punta)* to front and right side of placed left foot. Repeat on right foot.

Then prepare arms: Bring right arm up slowly with eye-to-arm focus; left hand rests at waist with fingers together, pointing front. This positioning of feet and arms is used for transitions. (Remember the energetic lift of knee and skirt for changes in feet position.)

a. Maintain position and move head in toward the left shoulder and out toward the right elbow, and repeat 10 times increasing in momentum.

b. Maintain position and move head with hand (forearm at elbow) to the inside (left) and to the outside (right), repeat 10 times increasing in momentum.

c. Complete by bringing right arm down center to right side waist; eyes follow arm leftward and then rightward. Left arm is brought up overhead at ear level. (Make change to left foot.)

d. Move left arm out to right, down and around over feet and up, defying gravity with lift of arm/torso/head; control buttocks and abdomen, pulling body in and up. (Repeat 3 times.)

e. Complete by bringing left arm down center to left side waist; eyes follow arm rightward and then leftward. Right arm is brought up overhead at ear level. (Make change to right foot.)

f. Move right arm out to left side, down and around over feet and up, defying gravity with lift of arm/torso/head; control buttocks and abdomen, pulling body in and up. (Repeat 3 times.)

g. Complete by bringing right arm down center to right side waist; eyes follow arm leftward, then rightward. Both arms are brought up together. (Make change to left foot.)

h.   Move both arms together out to right side, down and around over feet and up, defying gravity with lift of arms/torso/head; control buttocks and abdomen, pulling body in and up. (Repeat 3 times.)

i.   Bend to the left side front at waist and back up to center slowly (2 times). Keep arms rounded, in extended arc to the left.

j.   Bend backwards to the left and straighten up slowly (2 times.)

k.   Bring both arms down on outside, in rounded arc, elbows held to waist level, palms inward.

l.   Change: Palms in/out (2 times).

m. Change: One palm in and one palm out, reversing in/out (2 times).

n. Lift both arms up on outside in rounded arc, elbows held, with palms out.

o. Rapidly change positions of hands: palms in/palms out, (4 times). Then pose, creating an expression in fingers of hands.

5. Positions of the Arms
(Las Posiciónes de los Brazos)

a. With left foot extended, bring both arms up center, with strong energy, lifting with elbows. Pose, with energy extended to fingertips. Bring both arms to the back and hold pose.

b. Change to right foot, at the same time extending both arms out, moving forward. Extend energy to fingertips and hold pose.

c. Simultaneously change to left foot and bring left arm angled at chest level, with right arm to back, mid-spine (without touching body). Focus pose on left elbow.

Change to right foot and repeat the same on right side, right arm lead. Focus energy on right elbow and pose.

d. Simultaneously, change to left foot, bringing left arm angled at chest level and the right arm up above head, at ear level. Pose with focus on left elbow. (Spanish 3rd Position)

Change to right foot and repeat the same on right side, right arm lead. Focus energy on right elbow and pose.

e. Simultaneously change to left foot and bring both arms up together, above head, ear level. Pose, extending energy to fingertips, creating an expression in fingers of hands.

f. Simultaneously change to right foot, bringing right arm up and slightly at diagonal so that eyes focus on palm, while left arm assumes position at left side waist, not touching body.

Repeat the same on left side, with left foot and arm change.

g. Turn diagonally left and drop left arm and right arm to sides of body respectively. Shift weight from left to right foot, positioning right foot on ball of foot. Then bring both arms up center, gradually straightening knees (angled out and bent in *demi-plié*), and continue over head and down sides to waist, pulling torso up, inclining body left and front. Conclude with hands at waist and simultaneous accent of head up and in attitude. (Progression)

h. Repeat a, b, c, d, e and f, using *filigranas*.[1] Repeat using *filigranas* and move forward with each change on left or right side.

6.   Movements of the Arms (Baile de Brazos)

a. Set (1) (Arms down on outside and up on outside)

Direction: (L) left diagonal
              (R) right diagonal
              (F) front

Preparation: (See #4 to review positioning of foot to begin the study.) Lift right arm from waist, above head at ear level. Repeat on left side. Both arms are up above head at ear level to start. While one directed arm moves, the other remains posed and stationary.

---

[1] *Filigranas*, see Appendix, page 63

Movement (R):	Looking right, bring right arm slowly down on the outside of the body to waist (palm up and out, then midway turn palm down toward ground) then back up above head at ear level.

Transition:	Make weight change on right foot; lift left foot turning left.
Movement (L):	Repeat the same on left side as in Movement (R).

Transition:	Looking right, make weight change and face forward.
Movement (F):	Facing forward, in Spanish 3rd position – with right foot out. Bring both arms down slowly on the outside of the body to waist, looking right.

Transition:	Change to left foot, in Spanish 3rd position – with left foot out, looking left.

Movement (F):	Bring both arms up above head at ear level.

Close:	Bring both arms down slowly to waist and hold pose with hands properly placed.

Apply *filigranas* to above movements (R) (L) (F).

Start with warm ups: *filigranas*

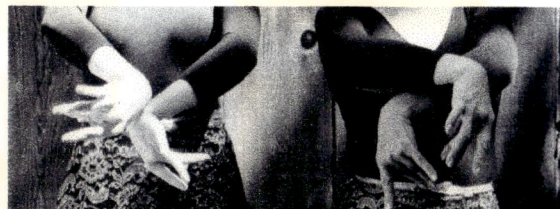

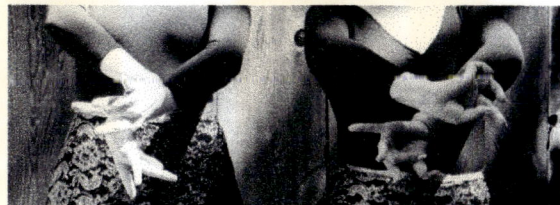

a. Rotate only wrists (fisted) in/out.

b. Extend energy from hand to finger tips, and hold fingers slightly apart, rotating them in/out using a lead finger. (For male dancer's hands use closed finger formation, rotating as a unit, "*Escudero styling*".)

c. With right foot in Spanish 3rd Position, move both arms and hands together, going in opposite directions from center. The right arm moves up at a diagonal on the right side while left arm moves to the left side, at waist.   Both hands form *filigranas* as the arms move and lift to respective positions. (Repeat to self: "right hand over left, fingers and wrists rotate in/out. Oppose fingers and rotate wrist in/out. Move right arm at diagonal and left arm to left side. Rotate wrists in/out. Hold right arm up and focus on right hand as left arm and hand pose at left side. Repeat fully on left side (change to left foot, 3rd position).

b. Set (2) Arms down out outside and up on inside.

Directions: (R)(L)(F)

Preparation: Same as Set 1, starting right.

Movement (R):   Looking right, bring right arm down on the outside of the body slowly to waist (forearm with open palm, changing midway with elbow pointed up and palms of hand toward ground. Bring right arm in and up center with left arm to pose.

Movement (L):	Repeat on left side as in Movement (R).

Transition:	Same as Set 1, going left.

Transition:	Same as Set 1, full front.

Movement (F):	Facing forward in Spanish 3rd position, with right foot out. Bring both arms down to waist, look right.

Transition:	Change to left foot, in Spanish 3rd position, with left foot out, looking left.

Movement (F):	Still facing forward, bring both arms in and up center slowly to pose above head, focusing on the hand-arm movement upward.

Close:	Bring both arms down on the outside slowly to release at both sides of body.
Variation (1):	Facing forward, looking right, right foot forward, bring both arms down on the outside of the body. Change to left foot while bringing left arm back and around to the left side from mid-back or kidney area.
	Change back to right foot while bringing right arm back and around to the right side from mid-back or kidney area. Continue both arms up center and pose above head, at ear level.

Variation (2): Facing forward, looking right, right foot forward, bring both arms down on outside of body. Change to left foot while bringing both arms up together at sides of the body to back of neck/hair, and up above head to assume pose with fingers out, back of hands at wrists touching.

Variation (3): Facing forward, looking right with right foot forward, bring both arms down on outside of body then up sides of body to face/profile. Continue both arms up above head to assume pose with fingers out, back of hands at wrists touching.

Maintain right foot forward and look straight ahead, bringing both arms down on the outside slowly to release at sides of the body.

Apply filigranas to above movements (R)(L)(F).

Start with warm-ups: filigranas

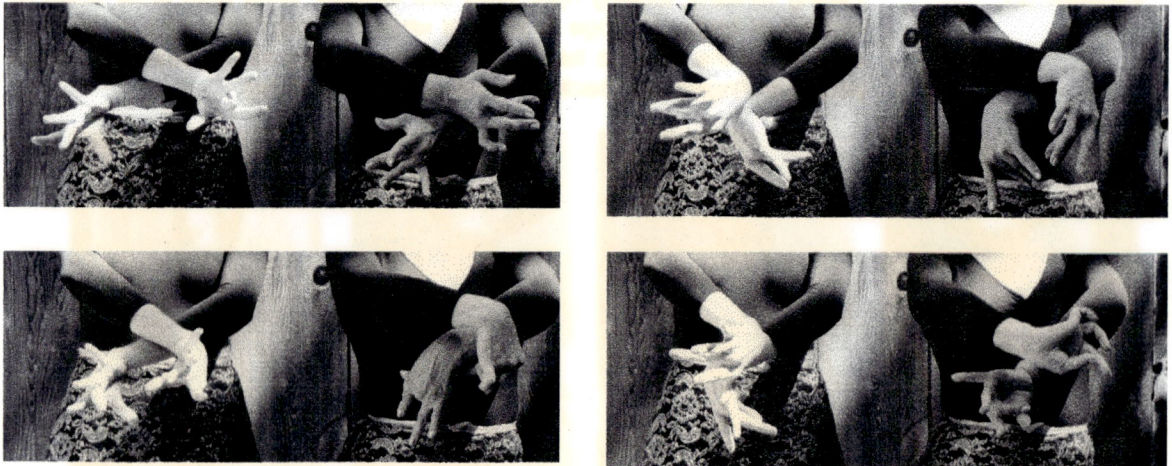

c. Set (3) (Arms down center and up on outside)

Directions:	(R)(L)(F) diagonals
Preparation:	See Set 1, starting right.
Movement (R):	Looking right, bring right arm down center to waist level, then back up on outside of body, above head, at ear level, to pose.

Transition:	See Set 1, going left.

Movement (L):   Looking left, bring left arm down center to waist level, then back up on outside of body, above head, at ear level, to pose.

Transition: See Set 1, full front.

Movement (F):   Facing forward, looking left with left foot out (Spanish 3rd Position) start left arm down center, followed immediately by right arm to waist level. Pose right arm and hand in space at waist as left arm continues up on left side of body above head and poses. Follow with right arm brought up on outside of body, above head to pose together with left arm. (Repeat Movement (F) on right side.)

33

Close: Bring both arms down on the outside slowly to release at sides of the body.

Apply *filigranas* to above movements (R) (L) (F).

Start with warm-ups: *filigranas*.

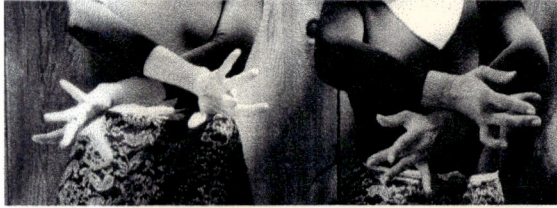

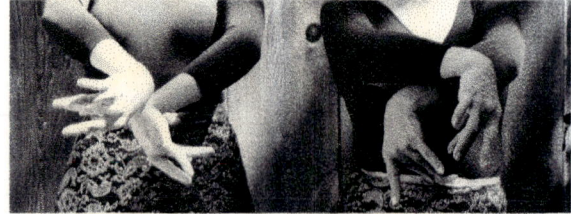

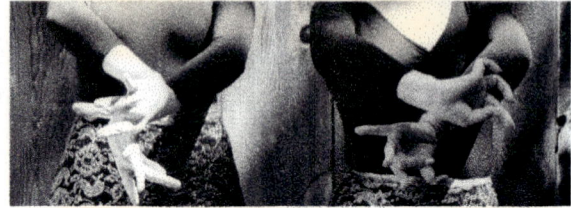

LAO-TZU

A good traveler has no fixed plans
And is not intent upon arriving.
A good artist lets his intuition
Lead him wherever it wants.
A good scientist has freed himself of concepts
And keeps his mind open to what is.

Thus the Master is available to all people
And doesn't reject anyone.
He is ready to use all situations
And doesn't waste anything.
This is called embodying the light.

What is a good man but a bad man's Teacher?
What is a bad man but a good man's job?
If you don't understand this, you will get lost,
However intelligent you are.
It is the great secret.

"Jesus, Isabel, why can't you just grab the bar like everyone else?"

Flamenco even inspires cartoon humor as in this clip from the New Yorker, brought by an excited student after her breakthrough in arm work : *Baile de Brazos*

Line and Laterality

... The *duende*, then, is a power, not a work.
It is a struggle, not a thought.
I have heard an old maestro of the guitar say:
"The *duende* is not in the throat;
the *duende* climbs up inside you,
from the soles of the feet."
Meaning this: it is not a question of ability,
But of true, living style, of blood,
Of the most ancient culture,
Of spontaneous creation.

Federico García-Lorca
(circa 1925)

IV. TECHNIQUES OF *BAILE FLAMENCO-JONDO*

A. Workshops

1. **Workshops I, II, and III** will be conducted in the techniques of *baile flamenco-jondo*. Ideally, the workshops will be no larger than twelve students and no smaller than six.

2. **Workshop I** will present the basics of line, foot placement and footwork *(taconeo)*, hand and arm movements *(baile de brazos)*, and the dance from the chair *(baile de silla)*. Short estudios or studies of the dance movements and footwork passages will be taught for *alegrías*, *soleares*, and *siguiriyas*.

3. **Workshop II** will feature use of the costume with a long train called the *bata de cola*. Included in this study will be the playing of tiny castanets *(palillos)*, and development of finger snapping *(pitos)*. The context will be the *siguiriyas* and *soleares* exclusively.

4. **Workshop III** will demonstrate interface skills for the dancers, singers/reciters, and guitarists in varied performance atmospheres *(ambiente)* such as concerts, private performances, indoor and outdoor venues, museum, restaurant, hotel and nightclub formats *(zambra/cuadro/tablao)*. There will be an opportunity to study *jondo* and *flamenco* styling and learn to use them tastefully in appropriate settings. This workshop will explore *flamenco* dance programming, costuming, and cliché versus creativity.

B.   Workshop I: Goals and Content

1. Expose the dancer/student to a new dance philosophy, technique and experience.

2. Cultivate a healthy respect for body intelligence in ourselves and others.

3. Interface responsibly with each other, helping where appropriate and asking necessary questions.

4. Relate past dance experiences to the current workshop, then apply these new learnings to future dance endeavors.

5. Allow time in the workshop for group reviews, small group practice sessions, and teacher-student attention.

6. The dancer/student will be exposed to the following *jondo* principles:
    - Focus and concentration
    - Individual energy flow
    - Control of body
    - Use of emotion as a dance technique
    - Rhythms, counts, accents, and musical phrasing in dance
    - Tension and relaxation
    - Poses and posturing (static and moving)
    - Fine muscle expression
    - Improvisation within the count or rhythmic pattern *(compás)*
    - *Jondo* as a survival kit: ¡aquí estoy yo!

7. Dance from the Chair *(Baile de Silla)*
    - Translate *baile de brazos* from standing to seated positions (posture and leveling)
    - Move to the *compás* of the *soleá*
        - Routine 1 ends with a break *(desplante)* for *soleá*
        - Routines 2 and 3 demonstrate rising from the chair enter standing dance model

8. Movements for Dances *(pasos/paseos)*
   - Siguiriyas – *paseo* with *desplante* and use of finger snapping (*pitos*)
   - Soleá – *pasos* to demonstrate levels and torsion
   - Alegrías – *pasos* to El Estampío and Rosa Durán's *desplante*

9. Footwork for Dances *(taconeo/escobilla)*
   - *Siguiriyas – escobilla* styling
   - *Soleá – taconeo* styling
   - *Alegrías – escobilla* styling

10. Accompaniment
   - Guitarist and singer/reciter accompany practice of *baile de silla* movements, and footwork for the s*iguiriyas, soleá* and *alegrías*

C.   Definition of *Jondo*

Jondo means deep, profound, and heartfelt. According to Caballero Bonald (1959), *jondo* is an ivory tower, not a closed circle. It is a way of life through an art form that interprets the popular spirit and emotional range of the group, while linking the mysterious with the expressible. *Jondo* dancing is without set geographical boundaries, although it came to life in the particular *flamenco* schools of Seville, Cádiz, and Granada. It has been the vision and mission of individual dancers to establish valid standards of execution in their dance creations, and to institute their own personal styles as with El Raspao's *Zapateado*, the *Rosas* of Miracielos, Joaquin el Feo's *Tienetos*, Vicente Escudero's *Siguiriyas*, La Mejorana's *Soleares*, the *alegrías* of El Estampío and Isabel Santos, and the *jondo* dances of Rosa Durán. Everything depends on the dancer's knowing how to use his or her apprenticeship of styles, then forgetting them to allow the language of movement to take over. The *jondo* dancer makes full use of inspiration and intuition to attain unpredictable inventiveness in the dance.

There is an unmistakable *jondo* expressiveness called *duende* or sprightliness that possesses the performer and the performance. *Duende* happens without warning during the artistic struggle between remembering and forgetting, perfection and imperfection. A spirit ally or friendly demon descends upon the dancer to dance with him or her, transcending time and space in a whimsical encounter.

Certain *jondo* dances, songs, and guitar accompaniment are considered *jondo* because of the styling, sentiment and intensity they are expressing. However, *jondo* can be experienced at any given moment, and one can never say that such a song, or dance cannot become *jondo*.

D. Comparison of *Castanet* and *Jondo* Dancing

CASTANET DANCING	*JONDO* DANCING
• Uses *castanets*	• Uses no implements; Rosa Durán played *palillos* to imitate tongue-clicking and finger snapping rhythms
• Danced by couples or *corp de ballet*, orchestrated, or with several guitarists	• Solitary dancer, with or without guitarist, singer or reciter
• Requires ample space and staging	• Limited space no props
• Dancing is mobile, gymnastic, light, upbeat, accompanied, with clapping and agile capers	• Static, somber, undulating, trance-like, cadenced, restrained, understated
• Speeded *compás* and increased tempo	• Modulations of tempo; strict adherence to *compás*
• Focused use of legs and entire body; fewer isolations	• Extended and accented use of torso, arms, and hands; many isolations
• Use of *castanets* and footwork together; active body participation	• Alternating simple and intricate footwork with nuances of sound and tempo; rest of body postured, sympathetic
• Colorful costuming with flare and flounce	• Black, solid colors with polka-dotted, floral accents
• Dancing contains concrete images linked by preconceived patterns, evoking expectations	• Language of the dance is symbolic, abstract, mysterious, dependent on dancer's inner resources
• Extroverted performance	• Introverted performance

JONDO EXPRESSION DURING DANCE AND GUITAR DIALOG

E.   *Flamenco* Dancing

Flamenco dancing is a bifurcation of *jondo* and historically, it shares a *jondo* inheritance. However, *flamenco* dancing can become excessive through the use of fancy footwork and turns, speedy *compás*, and sensational costuming and staging. In much of modern *flamenco* dancing, the *jondo* orthodoxy is lacking. *Flamenco's* popularity and attractiveness, made evident by competent and artistic performers in varied formats, have given it the semantic umbrella under which light *(chico)* and *jondo* dancing reside. Individual *flamenco* dances are often referred to as *chico, intermedio*, or *grande*, depending on the emotional, technical, and stylistic delivery of the piece.

F.   Summary

The *jondo* arts of dance, poetry, song, and guitar music reflect traditional values and renew the historical and spiritual survival of the group, as in the case of the Spanish Gypsy, descendants of East Indian tribes seeking basic freedoms. *Jondo* dancing is the least commercial of the Andalucian dance heritage and the most difficult to master because of its precision of line, nuances, adherence to the *compás*, and emotional intensity.

G.   References

Borrow, George. *The Zincali, An Account of the Gypsies in Spain*. 1908.
Caballero, Bonald, J.M. *Andalusian Dances*. 1959.
Claramunt and Albaicin. *El Arte del Baile Flamenco*. 1977.
Clébert, Jean-Paul. *The Gypsies._*1967.
De la Peña, T.M. *Teoría y Practica del Baile Flamenco*. 1969.
Duff, Charles. *A Mysterious People*. 1964.
Esty, Katherine. *The Gypsies: Wanderers in Time*. 1969.
Quintana, Bertha. *Qué Gitano! (Gypsies of Southern Spain)*. 1963.
Starkie, Walter. *Don Gypsy*. 1937.
Starkie, Walter. *In Sara's Tents*. 1953.
Tomãsevíc and Djuric. *Gypsies of the World*. 1988. ISBN: 0-8050-0924-8
Tong, Diane. *Gypsy Folktales*. 1989. ISBN: 1-56731-105-9
Yoors, Jan. *The Gypsies*. 1967.

V.   FANS AND SHAWLS IN SPANISH *FLAMENCO* DANCING

A.   Chinese Origin

The prototype of the Spanish fan and shawl originated in China, soon after the introduction of silk in about 1900 BC, and embroideries as early as the Five Dynasties, AD 907-960. During the Moorish occupation of Spain, trade and travel from China and India brought silks and spices, and for more than 400 years, the Mediterranean Jews had conducted trade with the Khazars in Southeastern Russia, a half Mongolian people who converted to Judaism. Fans and shawls were also articles of trade brought back to Venice by Marco Polo and his nephew from the Chinese court and the Silk Road. The large, fringed shawls were re-introduced to Spanish culture by Magellan, from his contact with Chinese trading ships in Manila Bay. These large, fringed shawls from Shanghai became known as the *"Mantón de Manila."* Shawls adorned the upper class Mandarin with tassels and fringes, and embroidered silks became tapestries, symbolic decoration, coverlets, and outer garments.

B.   The Shawl as an Outer Garment

The shawl in Spanish culture is a diversified dress item. When worn as an outer garment or cloak it becomes the *"manto"* for men. The *"mantilla"* becomes a lacy head adornment for ladies. The flounces or *"volantes"* on dance skirts, and the long train on the *"bata de cola"* are variations of the shawl's dimensions. The aprons with lace work edgings on jota costumes are non-triangular little shawls tied around the waist with a ribbon. Ultimately, shawls of all sizes can be placed around the neck (with the "v" accented in the back), worn over the shoulder and pinned to the opposite side under the arm, draped over the chest and tied in the back, and hung at the waist with a loose knot or broach.   The Spanish shawl in

Flamenco dancing was also influenced by the settlement of East Indian Gypsies in the Iberian Peninsula. Like the Chinese shawl, the East Indian ones are embroidered, appliquéd, of silk or rayon, and variously fringed.

(The Rathistani and Lamani tribes were cotton weavers and trimmed skirts with colorful ribbons.) Both men and women adorned themselves with waist shawls, drape their elephants and horses with them, and used them as door curtains on their tents and caves.

C. Fans Adorned

Silk embroideries were used on hand fans with decorations of the four seasons and nature, or aspects of people in court or country life. The hand fan, usually made with scented woods or carved ivory, was an aesthetic and practical implement for keeping cool in warm climates and during long, hot summers. It was also a fashion, social class, and gender statement. In the 18th and 19th centuries, the opening and closing of the fan indoors and outdoors was the height of Parisian taste for elegantly dressed ladies. In Spain, Doñas in reserved, bullring seats waved their elaborate silk fans flirtatiously at five in the afternoon. In Chinese culture, men used fans of certain construction, in a prescribed manner, and for ceremonious occasions according to their class. The Chinese were the first recorded culture to use fans in their dances. Their earliest fans were ornamented and usually made of real peacock feathers. Today, the fan has been integrated into many dance cultures, namely Japanese, Korean, and Spanish.

The fan in Spanish culture and dance retains the Chinese form but has replaced textiles, materials, and designs to reflect the Iberian life. The dance fan is known as an *"abanico,"* and the large-sized fan is called a *"pericona."* When fans are not implements for the dance, they become framed art and collectibles, household decorations, or wall and window coverings.

D. Fans and Shawls as the Props of Mood and Romance in Dance

The role of fans and shawls in the dance is more than a colorful accent or flourish of technique. Effectively, they are extensions of the armwork and integrate with the articulations of the body to express a total balance of line. The fan and the shawl are manipulated with the fingers, hands and wrists, passing over, around, and with the moves of the dance choreography. However, both the fan and the shawl must be in concert with the theme, mood, and music of the dance. The following four dances describe the use of fans and shawls in their creative execution.

"A Dónde Va Bella Judia?*"* This *peteneras* uses a small hand fan and sets the mood of the dance with the seated dancer opening it gradually to a *soleares* count, creating an air of mystery and secrecy of the solo connection. The fan is used to hide the eyes as they survey their world, into which the dancer enters with the snap of a closed fan, thrown in the direction of the guitarist. Rising from the chair, the dancer continues the solo quest for her lover, wearing the large shawl crisscrossed over her chest and tucked in at the waist. The shawl work of the dance shows her weaving in and out of herself until she finally tosses it away and continues her romantic escape to the tryst. She moves furtively, as she is observed and followed by another on the cobblestones of a Cordovan *callejón*.

"Guajiras-Colombianas-a Carmen Amaya."
The guajiras is danced from the chair with a hand fan tucked in at the waist of the skirt. As the guajiras changes to a *Colombianas* and the song "por Carmen Amaya," the fan is lifted from the waist band and snaped open. It makes arcs and flourishes along with the undulations of the dance movements and accents the 6/8 rhythm. The opening and closing of the fan and its weaving articulations express a celebration of the self with flirtation and tropical sensuality.

"Romance de Amor." This dance utilizes classical, *flamenco*, and *escuela bolera* dance techniques in five movements or *coplas*. A large fan or *pericóna* tells the story of romantic love moving lyrically through five moods: the readiness; the contact; the flirtation; the embrace; and the recollection. The costume for the dance uses a *mantilla* fixed on the head of the dancer with a decorative comb or *peineta*. This is a variation of the small shawl and gives a touch of elegance and reverence to the whole affair.

"Choryu" (Multicultural/Ethnic), music by Kotoist, Kimio Eto. *Choryu* means the current and expresses the tide of human feelings from intense interactions to poised resignation. Japanese classical and *flamenco* dance techniques are melded into a choreography that utilizes the Japanese fan, the *"obi"* sash, *kimono* sleeves, *flamenco* skirt, and dance shoes. The fan dramatizes life's seasons and becomes a prop for water wheels, windmills, mirrors, and parasols. The *obi* sash is really a shawl that extends to the world from the waist of the dancer as it imitates the current, contained and moving.

E.   References

Air China. *China, Destination Manual.* Korea: Wilsted and Taylor, 1994.

Bruhn and Tilke. *Pictorial History of Costume.* New York: Arch Cape Press, 1988.

Campbell, J. and Moyers, B. *The Power of Myth.* New York: Doubleday,1988.

Collier, Jr., John. *Visual Anthropology: Photography as a Research Method.*
        New York: Holt, Rinehart, Winston, 1967.

Festival of India. *ADITI: The Living Arts of India.* Washington, D.C.: Smithsonian
        Institution Press, 1985-1986.

Hall, E. *The Silent Language (Map of Culture).* New York: Doubleday, 1981.

Hall, E. *The Hidden Dimension.* New York: Anchor Books, 1990.

Hall, E. *The Dance of Life.* New York: Anchor Books, 1989.

Hall, E. *Beyond Culture.* New York: Anchor Books, 1989.

Leach and Fried. *Standard Dictionary of Folklore, Mythology, and Legend.*
        New York: Harper and Row, 1984.

National Palace Museum Text. *Great National Treasures of China.*
        Taipei, Taiwan: 1983.

Storti , C. *Art of Crossing Cultures.* Maine: Intercultural Press, 1990.

Tomajevic and Djuríc. *Gypsies of the World.* New York: Holt, 1988.

Valdés, J.M. *Culture Bound* (Chapter 6). New York: Cambridge Press,1986.

Line and Laterality Revisited

VI. SCULPTURE, ART, AND ARCHITECTURE REFLECTED IN *JONDO-FLAMENCO* DANCE

From Asian cultures, specifically the East Indian and Chinese, we see in its sculpture, art, and architecture the prototypes of body line, centering, arm, hand, foot positions, and concentrated focus that reside in *jondo-flamenco* dancing. What we see in nonmoving forms is captured movement that is revealed in the dance through a sequencing of poses (*"posturas"*) and nonposes, a connecting of poses (*"pasos"*).

Early on, dancers danced at the doors of temples and on the floors of an inner sanctum, in an original and sacred language of the body called dance. Fundamentally, it was dancing from the inside out, with concentricity of inspired and cathartic movements and energy.

Sculptors, artists, and architects imitated these living models in their works, and even the embodiments of deities were imbued with both divine and earthly attributes.

The following illustrations from photos taken in the British Museum in October 1999 are captioned to show aspects of bodyline, centering, arm, hand, foot positions, and concentrated focus reflected in *jondo-flamenco* dance. Temple art and architecture from Hampi, Belur, and Halebeedu in South India are included and captioned to direct the reader to salient points of dance posture.

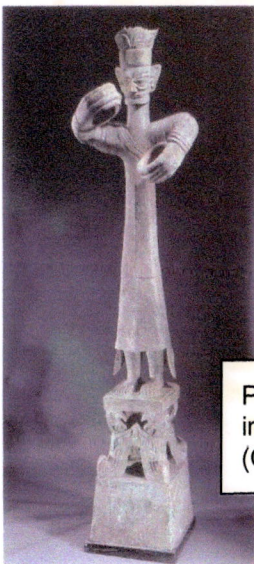

Head-to-shoulder attitude on body left, and geometry of right angles: chin, shoulders, elbow, knee, foot (Chinese).

Plasticity and geometry in eye-hand focus (Chinese).

Hand placements at waist and in air (*mudras*)* reflect body's energy flow and the story that it tells in contained movement (Chinese).

*In *flamenco*, "*mudras*" are positioned fingers of the hand to express completion of energy flow, a held movement in time, a transition, an abstracted emotional expression. The rotation of the wrist in and out with open fingers of the hand extended, is likened to the opening and closing of the lotus flower ("*loto*"), a metaphor for life's dawn and dusk, its yin and yang.

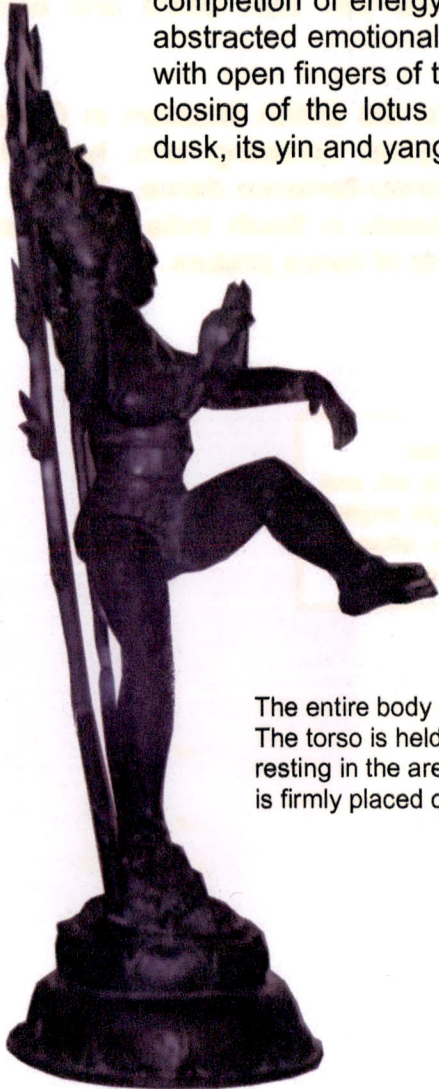

Laterality of head, shoulders, arm (elbow), hand (with *mudra* of protection), knee and foot in the posture of Shiva statue (the Nataraja aspect of the nine modes of dancing). Shiva's dance indicates a continuous process of creation, preservation, and destruction (East Indian).

The entire body extends upward and outward. The torso is held and pulled up as the body is centered, resting in the area of the solar plexus. The standing leg is firmly placed on the demon Apasmarapurusa.

Execution of shoulders, lift of left arm, its angle and focus, and position of knees and turned out left foot. Note also the torsion of torso responding sympathetically toward the intent of focus (East Indian).

Back of smallest figure in vertical, postured stance. Notice a controlled yet sensual articulation of the hands captured in the statue (East Indian).

Vertical position and centering. The arms are at the forehead above the eyes, and the hands indicate prayer or clapping pose (East Indian).

"Stilled motion" in sculpture. A *mudra* made at the left cheek of the dancer reflects fluid movement on the left side with slightly extended and lifted left foot leading the whole body in a circular way (East Indian).

Laterality of head, shoulder, arm, knee, and foot. Energy is focused and there is a facial expression of exquisite delight (East Indian).

Wall carvings on Holysaleswara Temple in Halebeedu show musicians and dancer. Note position of arms and castanet like instruments held in the hands.

"A dancing view" at Chennakeshava Temple (Belur, South India).

Natya Ganapathi (Dancing Ganesha) in Halebeedu (South India).

"The Shiva Dance" on Hoysaleswara Temple in Halebeedu (South India).

Belur temple carving of dancer with left foot turn out, torsion at waist, hip thrust, and hand in *mudra*.

Belur temple carving of dancer shows laterality, line, focus, and open third position (*flamenco*).

Execution of laterality. Head/eyes-shoulder-elbow focus, held expressions, knee twisted out, deep *pliés* (seated). Details of dancers in bas relief on a temple wall at Hampi (South India).

Bas relief in Hampi architecture shows "captured movement" with left laterality and focus, extension, and right knee turned out, with hip thrust.

Detail of dancer in bas relief at Hampi shows laterality of head, shoulders, arm, hand, knee and foot, and concentrated focus of the face.

Detail on stone figure at Hampi shows turn out of feet, arms above head at ear level, and a focused line.

Another attitude of raised arms, turned out feet, and torsion at waist with left hip thrust (used to execute *desplantes* or breaks in *flamenco*).

Sites
and
Atmosphere

VII. FLAMENCO AND THE JAPANESE INTERPRETATION

Setting the Scene of the *Flamenco* Dance Class in Tokyo

The way to Koenji, Tokyo, from the train station, is marked with small shops selling neat floral bunches, coffee houses with a student atmosphere, and one-car roadways connecting shrines, temples, and graveyards. On Sundays, the Komatsubara Spanish dancing group holds its classes. Three levels, all ages and sizes and three young men, scatter along the mirrors reviewing footwork, turns, and arm exercises. *Castanets* are warmed behind waistbands of skirts and jumpsuits and are soon clacking out of unison in the studio. In practice, the beginning students struggle at becoming centered and perfecting feet placement, the intermediate learners appear to use their hands too much or incompletely, and rather advanced ones still seek styling. When the head teacher, *Sensei* Kishi, appears, and the lady guitarist Toda is seated, a full hour's workout begins. Dance *routines or short dances - alegrías, soleares, bulerias, and sevillanas - are led by the sensei's* clapping of basic counts, *"ichi, ni, san..."* followed by arm exercises and *vueltas* (turns). Footwork and timing are corrected and heavily reviewed by the accentuated playing of the guitarist. The teaching of technique and sequential dance steps (choreography) is learned by continuous repetition, varied only by a distinctive teaching of the dance *compás*, or characteristic *flamenco* dance count.

Dancers and Instructors, Yoko Komatsubara and Kiyoko Kishi

Both Yoko Komatsubara and Kiyoko Kishi rely on their system of breaking down the counts, and placement of the feet. As a student in Spain, Miss Komatsubara had no time to analyze steps in class. Being without labanotation, (a system of dance notation), she committed these to memory and later worked them out. Since *compás* was hard enough for her to learn, she tried and perfected a system for her Japanese students which first involves a slow and careful verbal counting to dramatic placement of the feet, reinforced with guitar accompaniment. The *senseis* insist on *castanet* playing for accenting the *compás*, and stress its use in classical Spanish dancing.

Potential dancers for the performing group are selected from this class for body form, scholarship, interest, and the ability to learn patiently. Yoko Komatsubara feels she is a better dancer because she has taught. Through teaching, she can see flaws more objectively, learn something new, become inspired by another's dancing, and, test her own knowledge and confidence.

The trio of Komatsubara, Kishi and Toda, had its beginnings in an acting school where they were classmates. Miss Komatsubara's father was in the Kabuki Theater, her mother, a musician. She had studied classical ballet, then gravitated toward character, deciding finally to study *flamenco* because of its "dynamic" quality. Disillusioned with even the best instruction in Japan, she went to Spain to learn it authentically, and studied essentially with Pilar Lopez. Miss Komatsubara has made a tour of the Central and South American countries as a solo performer of *Ballet de Raphael de Cordova*. Since 1969, she has been presenting programs throughout Japan, with her company, *Ballet de Sol de España*.

Kiyoko Kishi spent twelve years studying Japanese classical dance and ballet, and trained later in Russia. She decided not to perform the genres professionally, because the classical ballet would be hampered by the "Japanese body type" which tends toward a longish torso and shorter, heavier calves. However, her impeccable ballet background reflects in her dance classes and she stresses it as basic to all dancing. In Spanish classical dancing and *flamenco,* the body turns and foot positions, especially third, are recalled from ballet. Fortunately for the trio and the school, she was moved by the intricacy of *flamenco*, and was taught Yoko Komatsubara's repertoire. Although *Sensei* Kishi enjoys a full schedule of teaching and choreographing programs, she loves to dance most of all.

Guitarist, Hiroko Toda

Hiroko Toda is rare among professional guitarists, being the only Japanese woman to play for *flamenco* dancers. Her musical studies were on the piano and violin, and she spent a year tutored by the brilliant Kenzo Takata. At twenty-eight, she began her own study of Spanish classical and *flamenco* guitar. Typically, Japanese guitarists study the music via recordings, in schools, or with solo teachers. This is the very opposite of guitar instruction in Spain, where one must attend an academy of dance and learn the *compás* first. *Sensei* Toda foresees a future of hard work, but is happiest playing for professional dancers and Theatre Flamenco. She is a very patient and helpful accompanist for students.

Some History

According to Miss Komatsubara, the first Japanese to perform in Spain was Masami Okata, who now resides there, employed as a secretary. The Japanese *flamenco* artists disbelieved the anecdote that brought me to Toyko, maintaining that since there is no strong unionism in Spain, dancers can find work. Our anecdotal *Flamenca* was provided a stage but was denied the supportive persons essential to flamenco communication. The moral of the anecdote is the ethnocentrism peculiar to those who guard the birthright of jondo, or soul of *flamenco*. Yoko Komatsubara describes jondo as a quality inherent in one of two classes of *cantos* or songs. The first, "*cante chico*," has a style and content expressing the delights of living. The second, "*cante grande*" can become jondo if it achieves "sprightliness," or transcends the heaviness of sorrow. Such song-poems of the gypsy race precede, accompany, or support the movements of the dancer, in the drama of earthbound footwork and skyward torso. It is a personal goal of Miss Komatsubara to be able to sing a Zorongo, which tells the old, sad story of the *gitano* (Gypsy) in prefacing the dance of the same name.

There is a spiritual affinity between *jondo* and Japanese classical dancing. Yoko Komatsubara refers to this affinity as a quality of "restraint," whereas the forms appear totally different. In the older gypsy dancing, there is a similar, inward style, a compactness of body, with arms opening outward and returning to a center. There are the common elements of stylized finger movements; accentuation of rhythms with foot sounds and props such as fans; feet placement, the conservation of space; and elaborate costumes with a *cola,* or train, as in *gagaku*, old court dancing, and the "*bata de cola*" of the *soleares* dance.

When exposed to Spanish and *flamenco* dancing, Japanese audiences showed an affection for the rhythms, and the color and pageantry of costumes and settings. There was also that popular confusion over the words "*flamenco*" and "*flamingo.*" *Flamenco* in Japan has a varied audience that is now catching on to the expressions of *jaleo* (verbal praises of the audience, clapping, and finger-snapping). A better understanding of the antique dialect of Andalucian Spanish would help the popularity of *flamenco*, especially its songs.

In Japan, *flamenco* is often considered a Spanish dance performed only in a saloon. Yoko Komatsubara has transformed *flamenco* for Japanese audiences, to the high level of the theatrical art. With the organization of her dancing team, and selection of a partner, Eduardo Monteros, (a protegé of Enrique el Cojo), Miss Komatsubara gave the first public performance on October 13, 1969, at Tokyo Sankei Hall, with dance director Victoria Eugenia. The repertory has been impressive: Lorca's *Boda de Sangre* (Wedding of Blood), Ravel's *Bolero*, Rodrigo's *Aranjuez*, a recital program, *Dance Dedicated to the Love of Mankind*, and Bizet's *Carmen*. *Carmen* has been the first of Miss Komatsubara's dream of adapting symphonic and operatic scores to Spanish dance. She had felt that the music of Carmen's Andalucian homeland and *flamenco*, best expressed her passionate world. Yoko Komatsubara, well known as "Tosa Niki," has no doubt attempted ambitious productions like *El Amor Brujo* and *La Vida Breve* with the integrity and knowledge of classical, folk, and flamenco forms. She has been awarded the highest recognition (*El Premio*) for her dancing ever given to a non-Spaniard, by the Spanish Government.

Spanish dancing teachers from Spain visit Japan to teach master classes. Matsuko O'Hashi sews the elaborately beautiful costumes for *Ballet de Sol de España*. The inseparable trio of Komatsubara, Kishi, and Toda, continue to admire Nureyev, Gades, and Cordova, while pursuing their hectic practice schedule in Koenji. And as very human persons who dance, they relax by loving to eat and to drink wine.

Appendix

"*Flamenco* Posture in the Insect World"

GENERAL FLAMENCO TERMINOLOGY

ARRANQUE (Pull up, uproot): The spontaneous and uncontrolled emotion which an artist may display at certain moments throughout the performance.

EL AGE OR ANGEL (Angel): Grace, good humor, friendliness, a certain way something is performed. It is like a spark, setting off an atmosphere that maybe merry, mocking or picaresque.

COBA (Flattery): A kind of eulogy or flattery, somewhat disinterested and less than sincere.

CORAJE (Courage): A way of performing the *toque, baile, or cante*, giving the impression of daring and courage.

DUCAS, DUQUELAS: Gypsy (Romany) for "sorrows."

ESTAMPA (Look, appearance): Refers to the stance, dance, form, and dress.

FLAMENCÓLOGO (Flamencologist): Someone who studies or investigates *flamenco*.

GUASA: An uncomplimentary word or deed, also a joke in bad taste.

JALEOS: Spontaneous exclamations of praise and flattery directed at the artist during his performance producing a more comfortable and encouraging atmosphere.

JARANA (Binge, space): People enjoying themselves while the singing and dancing is going on.

MAL AGE or ESABORIDO: Lack of grace and friendliness, sometimes with a bite of "*guasa*".

PALMAS (Hand claps): Rhythmic percussion performed with the palms of the hands. There are two types: high-pitched ("*claras*" or "*agudas*") and low-pitched ("*sordas*" or "*graves*").

PELLIZCO (Pinch): A way of singing, playing, or dancing which has a real bite to it, often charging the atmosphere of the performance.

REMATE: Conclusion of a musical or dance, phrase or series, but in a strong, decisive manner.

TERMINOLOGY TO DESCRIBE THE DANCING (*BAILE*)

BRACEO: Ornamental and expressive movements of the arms.

CAREOS (From "cara-face"): Characteristic step (*cara a cara*) found in the fourth of the sevillanas, where the couple's movements face each other, then pass to do a *"mata la araña"* (killing the spider) step.

CASTELLANAS or PASILLO: A combination of steps producing a walking movement found in the *alegrías*, for the *estribillo* or *canción* (chorus of song).

CASTAÑUELAS or PALILLOS (Castanets): Percussion instruments used to give rhythmic ornamentation in certain dances. Generally of wood, (pomegranate, *granadillo*), they are also made of compressed synthetic fiber (*fibrano/fibra*), plastic, and a mixture of wood and fabric (*tela*).

CIERRE (Close): The name for the *"llamada"* (consisting of one flat stomp of the foot) found in the *farruca* and *zapateado*, and used to close or conclude a particular section of the dance.

ESCOBILLA (Little Broom): The *zapateado* part of certain dances such as *alegrías, soleá*, and *farruca*.

FILIGRANA *(AS)*: The movement of separated fingers rotating from outside to inside and from inside to outside expressing a quality of enchantment. These filigreed movements of the hand have a cultural source in East Indian dancing and imitate the opening and closing of the lotus flower. The fingers and hands in *flamenco* dance have a life of their own.

GOLPE: Strong, hard stomp of a single foot (*planta*).

LLAMADA (Call) and **DESPLANTE** (Uprooting, a break): Rhythmic signals carried out by the dancer during the dance. The *llamada* is used to start or conclude a particular section, and is usually followed by a *desplante*, as a bold and virtuoso variation in footwork and posture. The order and placement can vary according to the choreography.

QUIEBRO (Dodge): The movement or posture of the body in a dance step, involving a bending at the waist.

PASO *(OS)*: A dance step; collection of dance steps.

PASEO: Walking, posturing steps accompanied by melody of music.

PITOS (Finger snapping): Percussive effective generally carried out with the thumb and middle finger of both hands.

TACONEO (*tacon* or *heel*): Execution of heel work.

ZAPATEAR: The carrying out of rhythmic percussion with the feet. Some of the various forms are listed below:

a)   **Escobillado** (from *escoba*/broom): The front part of the foot just grazes the floor, in forward and backward movements, imitating the movements of a broom.

b)   **Punta** (toes and front part of the shoe): Tap executed with the entire front part of the shoe, without using the heel.

c)   **Punta y Tacón** (toe and heel): Tap executed with the entire front part of the sole and following through with the heel.

d)   **Planta**: Execution of the whole of the foot on the ground evenly with varying speed and pressure.

e)   **Tembleque** (shaking): Performed *in situ* without displacement of the dancer by alternating taps of the right and left heels and the soles of both feet not moving at all.

f)   **Redoble**: *Plantas* executed evenly with the entire foot.

The above combinations are collectively known as

Zapatear, Zapateado, Taconear and El Taconeo.

TERMINOLOGY TO DESCRIBE THE GUITAR PLAYING (*TOQUE*)

AIROSO (Airy): An agile, rhythmically flexible, and elegant manner of playing.

ARPEGGIO: This is when the notes of a chord are played successively, normally from bass to treble, in various combinations.

ARRASTRE (Drag): The action of sliding a finger of the left hand from one note to another lending color and expression to the sound.

BONITO (Pretty, nice): Pleasant sounding, sometimes with a tendency to over sweeten the rhythmic and melodic passages.

CEJILLA (Barre): The position of the first finger of the left hand in holding down all six strings at the same fret is known as *cejilla*. It is represented by the letter "C". When it is only necessary to hold down three or four strings at a time the *media cejilla* (half *cejilla*) is used, this being represented by the letter "C" with a vertical bar through it: ₵. Roman numerals to the right of the "C" are used to indicate the fret behind which the finger is placed, C IV (*cejilla* at the fourth fret): C II (media *cejilla* at the second fret).

CHORD: This is a combination of notes played at the same time.

FALSETA or VARIATION: A nice, welcome variation played between verses in the song and at various times through the dance accompaniment, achieving variety in the dialog between the music of the guitarist and the movement of the dancer.

FINGERING: The system of numbers and letters used to indicate which fingers to use in playing a passage or an entire work.

FRÍO (Cold): Lacking in "bite" and "force."

GITANO (Gypsy) or **FLAMENCO**: Good playing with "bite" and "force."

LIGADOS: Notes are played with the left hand in ascending *ligados* (hammer-ons). The note is played by letting the finger fall, or "hammer" onto the fret where the next note is to be played. In descending *ligados* (pull-offs), the finger is raised or "pulled" off the previous note, letting the next or lower one, sound.

PASTUEÑO (Frank): Slow, calm playing.

PICADO: Playing a note to make it stand out. It is used in single-note passages as either parts of scales, melody line or counterpoint, is carried out by alternating the first and second fingers of the right hand.

POR MEDIO and POR ARRIBA: Expressions used by the *cantaor* to indicate which key he is going to sing in. *Por Medio* being the key in the Dorian mode whose dominant is A-major, and *Por Arriba* the Dorian key with E-major as dominant. The *cejilla* (capo) is used to change the key to suit the *cantaor*. (*Por Soleá al 5 Por Medio*: With the *cejilla* at the fifth fret, the *soleá* is played with chord positions corresponding to the key of D-minor (Dorian mode dominant of A-major), giving a real key of G-minor.) (*Por Soleá al 5 Por Arriba*: With the *cejilla* at the fifth fret, the *soleá* is played using A-minor chord positions (dominant E-major in the Dorian mode), giving a true key of D-minor.

PULSACIÓN: The way in which each guitarist actually plays the strings, from which his own characteristic sound is derived, in accordance with his technical ability and sensitivity.

SOBRIO (Sober): Measured, thoughtful, avoiding excesses. The content is serious and traditional.

SON (Sound): Describes the rhythm of a piece, kept by percussion (generally *palmas*) or simply the rhythm and *aire* of a particular style.

TIRO: The distance between nut and bridge saddle, which determines the tension of the strings.

TRÉMULO: Special effect produced by the repetition of notes played on the same string. There is one bass note *cinquillo* followed by four of the repeated treble notes.

TRINO (Trill): An ornamentation which consists of the rapid repetition of two consecutive notes.

VIRTUOSO: Total technical mastery correctly employed. When technical highlights predominate in all the pieces and in the way of playing, it leads to *"efectismo"* (ostentation, showing-off).

REFERENCES

de Larrea, Arcadio. *Guia del Flamenco*. Madrid: Editora Nacional, 1975.
    ISBN: 84-276-1223-0
Pohren, Don. *The Art of Flamenco.*
Starkie, Walter. *Spain, A Musician's Journey Through Time and Space, Vols. I, II.*
    Geneva, Switzerland: EDISLI...At Editions Rene Kister, 1958.

TERMINOLOGY TO DESCRIBE THE SINGING (*CANTE*)

AFILLA: Named for the great *cantaor* Francisco Ortega *El Fillo*. Term describes a horse, deep voice, occasionally abrasive but great depth.

AYES (Vocal sound, sung "ay, ay"): An expression that links the *tercios* and different styles within the same *cante*. They are also used to start or end a song.

DESGARRADA (Torn): A kind of voice broken up by feelings of abandonment and daring.

DOBLE or CAMBIO: The part of the song which is the most wrought out, uncontrolled, and dramatic.

ECO or RAJO: The particular sound characteristic of an individual voice related to "timbre" in music.

FALSETE: A voice higher in pitch than the normal voice, produced by a closure of the glottal gap while singing. Also known as *voz de cabeza* (head voice).

FUELLE: Capacity to link two tercios without taking breath. Also known as *tener poder* (having power).

JIPIO: An expression from Andalucia and Cartagena, originally a derivation of *hipar* - to hiccup; *hipido* hiccuped, meaning moan or whimper. It refers to moments in the *cante* when the singer's cry is interrupted or broken by a strong expression of pain or sadness.

LAINA: Fine, thin, generally brilliant in tone and in a high register.

MACHO: The name given to certain *cante*, for its energetic and spirited qualities, and used as a *remate* to conclude another. Some *machos* have become almost standard practice in certain styles, such as the Siguiriya de Maria Borrico, or used as a *remate* in serranas, and the soleá.

MECER EL CANTE (Rocking the song): Describes the slight oscillations in rhythm and volume practiced occasionally during the *cante*.

MELISMAS: Groups of ornamentative notes sung around the same syllable.

RECOGER LA VOZ (Collecting the Voice): The act of stopping the voice dead without making the slightest sound, only to start again at will.

PASTOSA (Pasty): Soft, smooth, with no peaks, pleasant to hear.

RECIA (Stiff): Strong, solid, but hard and rigid.

REDONDA (Round): Lacking in bass, full of trebles, and good sounding.

SALIDA (Exit): When the *temple* is of long duration or great virtuosity.

TEMPLARSE, TEMPLE (Tempering, tuning): Putting the voice in tune with the guitar as a prelude to starting the *cante*, to warm up the voice, with or without guitar accompaniment.

TERCIO: A melodic phrase, normally sung without pausing for breath.

REFERENCES

Grande, Felix. *Memoire del Flamenco, Vols. 1 & 2.* Espasa Calpe, S.A.:
    Selecciones Austral, 1999. ISBN: 84-239-1999-4
Hect, Paul. *The Wind Also Cried.*
Lorca, Federico García. *Poema del Cante Jondo.* Losada, S.A.:
    Buenos Aires Editorial, 1957.
Lorca, Federico García. *Romancero Gitano y Poema del Cante Jondo.*
    Madrid, S.A.: Espasa Calpe, 1980.

¡Con calo!   ¡Vamos allá!

FLAMENCO JALEO

(Words of Support and Encouragement[1])

1. General (All Purpose)	Translation
¡Vamos allá! (a Vamo ya!)	Let's get/go there!
¡Qué Gitana! or ¡Qué Gitano!	How Gypsy! What a Gypsy!
Tiene la gracia.	You have grace. You are graciousness/amusing.
¡Oye!	Listen!
¡Olé!	Interjection of "well done", "jolly good" and "bravo"!
¡Ozu!	An exclamation (mispronunciation of "Jesus")
¡Oju!	An exclamation (mispronunciation of "Jesus")
¡Vale!	Worth it!
Vino y Rosas y Aire	Wine, roses and character
¡Aire!	A sincere *jondo* or gypsy compliment. "It's all there". "You have it". "You have the aspect", "the look", "the essence". Used especially for the expression of *compás*, self-expression, and making the air move around oneself "giddy".
¡Guapa!	Beautiful! A compliment to a woman.
¡Guapo!	Handsome! A compliment to a man.
¡Aquí, Estoy Yo!	Here I am! (affirmation of performer/self/presence)

2. Footwork (Dance)	Translation
¡Así se baila!	Way to dance!
¡Toma, toma - toma te!	Take it away!
¡Agua, agua!	Water, water! (Thirsty from good, hard dancing.)
¡Como así, así!	It's like that!
¡Ay, caramba!	Exclamation equal to "holy smoke!"
¡Que salero tiene!	You have the flavor!
¡Por hay (ay)! or ¡Vaya!	That's the way!
¡Baila bien!	You dance pretty! You dance well! You dance nicely!
¡Baila bonita/bonito!	

---

[1] (Words of support and encouragement during a performance)

3. Guitarist

Spanish	Translation
Así se toca la guitarra de España.	The way to play the Spanish guitar.
Así se toca eso ...	That's the way to play that…
Toca bien, toca bonito.	You play well; You play pretty.
Toca, gitano..	Play, gypsy ...
Anda, niño, niño de _____	Come on child (guy) child of _____ (name of place or origin)
Anda, niña, niña de _____	Come on child (gal), child of _____ (name of place or origin)

4. Singers, Reciters

Spanish	Translation
¡Anda, canta bien!	Come on, sing well! Sing pretty!
¡Canta bonito!	
¡Con calo!	With gypsy style!
¡Así, se canta eso!	Way to sing that!
¡Ay, simpática (simpatía)!	Pleasant! Sympathetic! Attractive!

5. Singers, Reciters to Dancers

Spanish	Translation
Ya no se llaman dedos los de tus manos que se llaman claveles de cinco ramos.	The fingers of your hands are more like five bouquets of carnations.
Cuatrocientos contadores se a contar las gracias de tu hermosura no pudieron acabar.	400 accountants could not finish counting the graces of your beauty.

¡Guapo!

¡Ay, caramba!

Required Clothing and Dress Code
(for *Flamenco* Dance Class)

I. **Reasons**

    A. It is the direct expression of the culture of the dance you have chosen to study. *Flamenco* is Spanish, and its cultural roots are both occidental and oriental. The Hindu-Bayadere, Indian-Asian dress orthodoxy shows restraint and a range of styles and colors appropriate to the occasion reflecting femininity, masculinity and self-expression. It is also designed for certain activities such as secular and nonsecular dances. Spanish dance academies, professionals, and the *jondo*-lineage adhere to acceptable standards of dress that respect this dance art.

    B. Both large and small muscle groups in the upper body and arms, legs and feet are going to be exercised and are therefore susceptible to changes in temperature through use/disuse, warming up and cooling down.

    C. With similarity in class dress, more attention can be given to learning and to individual movement and expression.

    D. _____

        (your reason)

    E. Necessary dance implements such as the *Mantón de Manila* (large shawl), *pericona* or *abanico* (fans), and *castañuelas* or *palillos* (castanets) should be kept handy in a tote bag or carrier with the rest of your dance clothing and shoes for class.

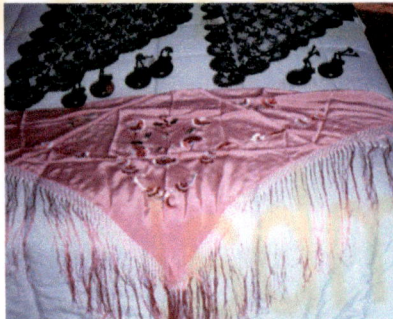

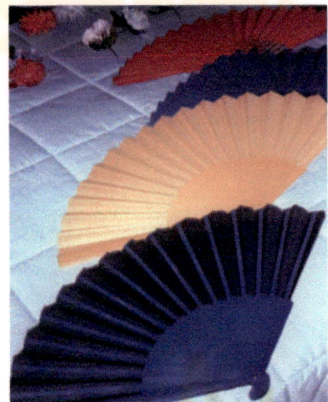

72

II.   Requirements

A.   Both male and female students should adhere to personal hygiene per the social contract in dance/physical education in the studio classroom.

B.   Torsos should be fully covered, with neck and hands exposed. Color and style of leotard, shirt, blouse, etc., is your choice. Black is preferred because it complements line and focuses on dance movements.

C.   Pants, catsuits, and practice skirts should be ankle length and roomy enough for freedom of movement or use as a dance technique. Color and style are your choice.

D.   Tights and leg warmers during rigorous workout, and a shawl or wrap to cover up when cooling down or stopping activity during class for a short break are necessary. Tights or socks/stockings worn with shoes ensure foot health during class, and care should be taken to air out or wash and dry clothing with the closest contact to the body after each class.

E.   Shoes should be the regulation Spanish-Flamenco ones, ranging in material (ante/suede, cuero/leather; style (estilo Mercedes/Amaya); color (black, red, purple, tan); and heel height (1-7/8" − 2 − ½") tapered or cubed). (Maintain interior of shoes with foot sprays and powders, and frequently change inner soles.)

F.   Do not overspend. Haunt the discount clothing stores, second-hand and thrift shops. With proper student ID, you can request a discount at dance wear and retail outlet stores.

Workshop in Stage Makeup Application
Presented by: Paula Ann Reyes.[2]

Tools: Large brush for powder and other makeup
Contour brush
Eyebrow brush
Group of tiny brushes (used for shadows and liners)
Tiny flat brush for lips
Lip pencil in different colors (black, brown or red)
Spatula applicator
Point tip applicator
Little cotton balls
Sponges (triangular, sea sponge)
Cheek color
Eye shadows of various colors (use shades to match your complexion)
Clown white makeup or soft white eyeliner pencil
False eye lashes and glue
Eyeliner (liquid or pencil)
Foundation or base
Loose powder to match foundation or transparent/iridescent
Contour pencils
Concealer sticks (green/blue to reduce reddish skin tones, natural tone to reduce bluish skin tones)

You must first put on your costume; if you do the reverse, you will mess up your makeup! Test the makeup base on your neck to see if your foundation will work. If it is too red or orange, you should get a lighter shade, if it looks pasty or white you need a darker foundation.

1. Foundation: Apply to entire face including lips, eyebrow and eyelids. Also apply to neck all the way down to your costume line. Apply base in downward strokes on the neck and upward strokes on your face. Use your concealer stick to hide any imperfections on your face and neck, blending it in with a point tip applicator, then reapply foundation over it. DO NOT apply over foundation. Use iridescent powder to finish.

2. Cheeks: Apply blush midway from nose and up toward your ear. Then take a big brush to blend it in and up. If you want your face to look smaller, then apply the brush to different areas to give it that effect.

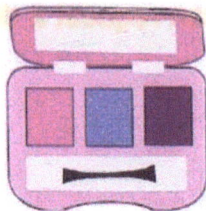

---

[2] Notes taken by: Samantha Luster, Seaside High School Dance Class, Seaside, California

3. Eyebrows: In measuring, use a thin brush and take it from the edge of your nose to the end of your eye. This is where your eyebrow should end. Always match eyebrow color with your complexion. Paint eyebrow in using small strokes going all the way across the eyebrow. You do not draw in the eyebrow.

4. Eyeliner: Need not be black all the time. For instance, if you are blonde and blue-eyed you may go with a gray instead. The darker your skin, the darker your color should be on the top of your eyes. Take your eyeliner 1/8 of an inch above the normal line of your eye, all the way to the corner and out. The bottom of your eyes, take the eyeliner a big away from the lash line using short strokes going all the way across to the corner and out. Never pull at the bottom of your eye.

5. Eye shadow: Put your highlighter color below the eyebrow line. Then your darker color goes around the orbit of the eye blended carefully. A light color can be applied to the area above eyelid.

6. Eyelashes: Remember that the way they are packaged is the way they go on your eyes. Do not close your eyes when putting on your fake lashes. You could glue your eye shut! If you have straight lashes, curl them before you put on your fake ones. All you need is a thin line of glue on the fake lashes to make them stick.   Then place your fake lash onto your eyeliner. Let it dry, then redraw your line. Match any lighter eyelashes to your fake ones. For the bottom, you can draw in eyelashes. Heavy perspiration often makes false lower lashes impractical as they will unglue readily.

7. Clown white: Put under eyebrow and between corners of the eye, inside, and a line out where your eyeliner has been drawn out.

8. Lipstick: Line your lips all the way around including the corners. You want to use brighter colors for stage so the people in the audience can see your lips!

Your makeup will be heavy but it is for the stage. Remember to always start with a clean face before applications. Always wash your face before and after every performance! If you look scary (in a matter of speaking) then it is all right for the stage! You want your chosen makeup colors to show.

(Men, I forgot you! Yes, you need to wear makeup for the stage, but just enough to get by. You want to wear foundation, eyeliner and lip color. You need not over-dramatize it. And depending on your complexion, you may also need a contour pen to hide any imperfections your skin may have.)

About The Author

From an early age, Alicia Morena studied in Hawaiian dance and classical ballet academies, and with international folkdance professionals in the Honolulu public schools. In the art of Flamenco and Spanish dance, she has studied at Estudio Calderón and Amor de Dios academies in Madrid, and trained with notable teachers Tossa Niki, Teo Morca, Lupe del Rio, Rosa Montoya, Rafael de Córdoba, La Tati, Maria Magdalena, Teresita Osta and Paco Romero. She is the protégé of Rosa Durán of Jerez and Madrid, a leading artist in the Jondo-Gypsy Flamenco lineage, who received awards for her dancing from heads of state in Spain, France, Italy, and the United States.

Alicia's signature programs feature traditional Flamenco choreographies and music that interface with the singing and reciting of García-Lorca poetry (Deep Song¡ Ay Córdoba!, Concierto Homenaje-a Lorca). Her choreographies are staged with ethnic and contemporary sculpture, original paintings, creative costuming, and photographic projections. She has performed, choreographed, and taught in California, Mexico, Hawaii, and Spain with her artistic partner, Roberto Andrés.

Alicia is the author and illustrator of Concierto Homenaje-a Lorca (interarts dance production), Tú y Yo (multicultural dance drama), and Tom-Boy, Aloha Girl, (a dance story for children), and Pilar's Magic Castanets (a dance drama set in Sevilla).

Alicia has been the recipient of grants from the Cultural Council of Monterey County (CCMC), the David and Lucile Packard Arts Initiative for the Community Foundation of Monterey County, the Monterey Cultural Arts Commission, and the Monterey Peninsula Volunteer Services (M.P.V.S.) on behalf of the Aditi Cultural and Charitable Foundation that she founded in 1999.

Acknowledgements

The author gratefully acknowledges the following people for their assistance in the creation of the 1st edition of the *Spanish Flamenco Dance Reference Guide*: Lauren Berreth-Vasseur for the initial graphics layout; Paula Reyes, Ann Malmuth-Onn, Dawn Sare, and Arline Young for professional input, proofing, and editing; Roderick Crawford for photo scanning; Mary Henness for final word processing and formatting of graphics with text; and, Sonia Sharma for making it happen legally.

Many thanks to those who helped me with the preparations of this, the 2nd edition: Rita Cummings for her word processing, formatting of graphics and desktop publishing assistance; Shane Rodarte for artistic touches to graphics; Kandas Nesbitt-Rodarte for consultation on graphic effects and coordinating and executing the guide's publication; Nancy McCreary, and Robert di Palma, for editing; Paula Reyes for professional content editing.

Mural by Marta Becket, Amargosa Opera House,
Death Valley Junction, California.

Photo Credits

Front Cover: (Audience Anonymous)
Alegrías: David Hayman
Bulerías: Theo Roberts
Farruca: Ted Cathey
Tango Gitano: Mal Wittenberg
Guajiras: J. Gentry
Jota Aragonesa: Robert di Palma
Peteneras: Mal Wittenberg
Romance de Amor: Walter Kool
Sevillanas Costume Design: Alicia Morena – di Palma
Siguiriyas: (Audience Anonymous)
Soleares: Mal Wittenberg
Tientos: (Audience Anonymous)
Black & White Dance Positions: Ignacio Ortíz
Photo Models: Marie Angrist and Dena Dawson-Crawford
Coro Gitano: Mal Wittenberg
Jondo Workshop Photo: Mal Wittenberg
Fans & Shawls: Robert di Palma; James Le; Mal Wittenberg; and Paula Cathey
India: Alicia Morena – di Palma
Japanese Artists: Gift to Alicia Morena – di Palma
Back Cover: Walter Kool

Student Reviews

"...complete and well organized from history of the art... performance guidelines—costuming and make-up for the stage."

- Flora Anderson, Flamenco Dance Student

"...interesting and informative... an explicit instructional guide to the technique of the flamenco dance and reflects the author's passion and precise technique, both of which cannot be compromised in the dance."

- Linda Bannister, Flamenco Dance Student

"Knowing the background of any cultural expression is extremely important in understanding how the soul of the dance is to be communicated, and the historical portions of the book gave me a much better appreciation for flamenco and those who practice it."

- Kevin Miller, Flamenco Dance Student

"...authentic and useful."

- Rosa Jong, Flamenco Dance Student

"Alicia goes through every move step-by-step."

– Angela Perez-Gray, Flamenco Dance Student

ORDER FORM

http://flamencoguide.com   **toll free fax: 877-612-8306**

Company Name: _____

Contact Person(s): _____

Phone Number: _____ Fax Number: _____

Email Address: _____ Purchase Order Number: _____

Billing Address	Shipping Address:

Discount (check one)	**Shipping and Handling**: *Orders are shipped USPS Media Mail or FedEx Ground. Domestic rate for* First Book $4.30; each additional Book: $.50 *International rate for First Book $9.00; each* additional book: $1.00 (U.S. Currency)
☐ Booksellers (40%) ☐ Libraries (25%) ☐ Bulk Order of 10 or more (25%)	

Quantity	Description	Unit Price	Total Price
	"Spanish Flamenco Dance Reference Guide 2nd Ed." by Alicia Morena - di Palma (ISBN 0-9729454-0-7)	$34.95	

Payment:		
☐ Check or Money Order ☐ Visa ☐ MasterCard	Less Discount	
	Shipping & Handling	
	Total	

Name on Card	**Card number**

Expiration Date	**3 Digit CVS (in signature line on back of card)**

Signature: _____ Date:_____

Order by Fax Toll Free: 877-612-8306   or by Mail: Wood Designs, Inc.
                                             Attn: Flamenco Guide
                                             PO Box 1790
                                             New Waverly, TX 77358